PRAISE FOR *STARDUST:*
'The depth and breadth of this truly imaginative and inspiring body of work reflects the different sectors of society and many regions and countries that have found their way to the University Centre Grimsby to compete in the Hammond House International Poetry Prize.'
Christopher Sanderson

'An imaginative and thoughtful collection of world poetry and songs reflecting a variety of cultures, styles and tastes, but always resonating with the universal truths that affect us all.'
Steve Jackson

'This superb anthology gathers some of the best in modern writing from around the world.'
Hugh Riches, Journalist and Broadcaster

'Inspiring lyrics, polished performances and imaginative production. A brilliant opening set for the first year of this new category.'
Rachel Makena, Singer-Songwriter

OTHER PUBLICATIONS:

Precious
Award Winning Short Stories

Precious
Award Winning Poetry

Shakespeare In Debt
by Ted Stanley

Who's Afraid Of The Dark – Not Me!
by Sarah Smith

Cows In Trees
by Julian Earl

The Dog With The Head Transplant
by Julian Earl

Leaving
Award Winning Short Stories

Leaving
Award Winning Poetry

Survival
Award Winning Short Stories

Survival
Award Winning Poetry

Stardust
Award Winning Short Stories

STARDUST
AWARD WINNING POETRY & SONGS
Edited by Ted Stanley

STARDUST
AWARD WINNING POETRY & SONGS

1st Edition published in the UK in 2022 by
Hammond House Publishing Ltd

ISBN: 978-1-7399985-1-6

The right of the individual writers to be identified as the author of this work has been asserted in accordance with sections 77 and 78 of the Copyright Designs and Patents act 1988.

All rights reserved. No part of this publication may be reproduced, stored in a retrieval system, or transmitted in any form or by any means, electronic, mechanical, photocopying, recording or otherwise, without the permission of the Publisher in writing.

Page Design by Alex Thompson
Proofreading by Jennie Liebenberg
Cover Design by Ted Stanley

Cover Image *STARDUST* by Deborah Geddes, first exhibited in 2021. Produced by permission of the artist.
All rights reserved.

The opinions expressed in this book are entirely those of the individual authors and are not endorsed or supported by the publishers or their sponsor, University Centre Grimsby.

Contains language that may be considered unsuitable for a younger audience.

Hammond House Publishing Ltd
13 Dudley Street, Lincolnshire
DN31 2AE, United Kingdom

www.hammondhousepublishing.com

STARDUST
AWARD WINNING POETRY & SONGS

Enjoy this eclectic collection of poetry and songs that brings together award winning writers from around the world.

STARDUST is the sixth in a series of poetry and song anthologies, each featuring a different theme and including the winning and shortlisted poems and songs from the annual *Hammond House International Literary Prize*.

Includes the winners of the
2021 International Literary Prize

The opinions expressed in this book are entirely those of the individual authors and are not endorsed or supported by the University Centre Grimsby.

Contents

Introduction | *Ted Stanley*	xiv
– Poetry –	
Playground | *Amanda Anastasi*	2
Light | *Alyxandria Arrowood*	4
Polaris | *Tamara Barrett*	6
Jupiter in Her Mind | *Alex Bassett*	8
Illuminated Destiny | *Susie Berns*	10
A Transformation | *Rachel Carney*	12
coal bunker, 1977 | *Teresa Cooper*	14
Reasons for Being There | *Jean Cooper Moran*	16
Star Dust | *Judith Drazin*	18
The Churn of Dreams | *Megan Easley-Walsh*	20
Spellbound | *Ruth Flanagan*	22
Summer Lightning | *Dagne Forrest*	24
Funfairness | *Nathaniel Frankland*	26
Stardust knows no bounds | *Mette Honore*	28
Shooting Stars | *Vera Ivanova*	30

Contents

Summertime Blues | *Steve Jackson*	32
The Pebble and the Pond | *Paul Jauregui*	34
A.I Robot Lover | *Anthony Leaman*	36
Birthday | *Róisín Leggett Bohan*	38
Back To The Garden (for Lucy) | *Mark Liston*	39
Native Stardust | *Patricia Anica Llorando*	42
Stardust | *Meg Macleod*	44
Hypnos and The Island Of Dreams | *Helen Marler*	46
Mount Saint Helen, May 18th 1980 | *Brittany Nohra*	50
Driving on Empty | *Mason Nunemaker*	52
Learning to Live | *Bradley Peters*	54
Fireworks | *David Punter*	56
What Matter That I'm Matter-Made | *Sheila Ronsen*	58
Carrying Black Holes | *Alicia Sometimes*	60
Heat Death of the Universe | *Alicia Sometimes*	62
My Little Girl | *Daniella Speirs*	64
Golden Boy | *Tim Taylor*	66

Contents

The Fixed Stars | *Tim Taylor* — 68

The Purpose of Moonlight | *David Terelinck* — 70

Eclipse | *Matt Wixey* — 72

Silent Running | *Roy Woolley* — 74

– Songs –

Woman in the Shadows | *Jean Cooper Moran* — 78

Hard To Sing My Song | *David Evardson* — 81

Lady of the Night | *Kirily McKellor* — 82

Bent, Bowed, Broken, Beautiful | *Kirily McKellor* — 84

Summer Blue | *Athanasia Teliou* — 86

Garage Days | *Matt Wixey* — 87

Recorded Songs — 90

Illustrations

Doriano Solinas	3
Meg Macleod	5
Glynne Bulman	7
Rachel Sene	9
Glynne Bulman	11
Margaret Inkpen	13
Glynne Bulman	15
Rachel Sene	17
Glynne Bulman	19
Doriano Solinas	21
Margaret Inkpen	22
Margaret Inkpen	24
Rachel Sene	27
Meg Macleod	29
Margaret Inkpen	31
Doriano Solinas	33
Meg Macleod	35
Doriano Solinas	37

Illustrations

Margaret Inkpen	39
Doriano Solinas	39
Glynne Bulman	43
Meg Macleod	45
Rachel Sene	46
Meg Macleod	51
Glynne Bulman	53
Rachel Sene	55
Glynne Bulman	57
Glynne Bulman	59
Glynne Bulman	61
Rachel Sene	63
Doriano Solinas	65
Glynne Bulman	67
Glynne Bulman	69
Doriano Solinas	71
Doriano Solinas	73
Meg Macleod	75

Acknowledgments

Alex Thompson, Deborah Geddes, Jennie Liebenberg, Leanne Doyle, Jonathon and Katherine Williams-Stanley and Richard Hall.

The University Centre Grimsby for sponsoring the International Literary Prize and the National Lottery Community fund for supporting our writer's groups. Competition Judges: Steve Jackson, Mason Nunemaker, Jean Cooper Moran, Rachel Makena and Cameron Richardson Eames.

The artists whose beautiful illustrations accompany the poems: Glynne Bulman, Rachel Sene, Margaret Inkpen, Doriano Solinas, and Meg Macleod.

Finally, all the writers who submitted such a wonderful collection of poetry and song. We are sorry we were unable to include more.

Introduction

Now in its 6ᵀᴴ year, the Hammond House International Literary Prize continues to attract some of the best talent from around the world, each writer interpretating the theme in their own unique way, often reflecting the diverse cultures, climates and communities of their homeland. Each year the standard becomes higher, challenging the judges – and making inclusion in the shortlist and this anthology an even greater achievement.

2020 was a year when we were focused on *Survival*. But, to help us look to a brighter future, a more inspirational theme was needed in 2021. *Stardust* was interpreted in so many different and imaginative ways by a new wave of emerging poets and songwriters – although a few familiar names made the poetry shortlist, displaying consistent quality in their writing. Some past poetry winners successfully turned their hand to song writing, our new category for 2021. It proved popular with both lyric writers and performers from around the world. The winners join our poets in this 2022 anthology.

We should never underestimate the power we have as writers to influence others and be a force for good. Is it the words of politicians that have influenced our own lives over the last 50 years, or is the storytellers, the songwriters, the poets, and the scriptwriters? Is it Thatcher, Farage and Trump, or is it Hemmingway, Dylan, Elliot, and Shakespeare? Martin Luther King's 1963 *I Have a Dream* speech changed the perception of the American civil rights movement forever. But these were not King's words; they were those of Clarence Jones, a political speechwriter and a poet.

As we stand at the threshold of the greatest challenge in the history of humankind, we have an opportunity and, dare I say, a responsibility as writers to make a difference on climate change. We can have more influence with the messages we weave into our poetry and our songs than the petulant preaching of politicians or the empty promises at climate conventions. Let your writing light the path to a brighter future, and don't let anyone crush your hopes, deter you from your dreams or steal the stardust from your eyes.

Ted Stanley

The cosmos is within us. We are made of star-stuff. We are a way for the universe to know itself.

Carl Sagan

POETRY

Shortlisted Entry

Playground
Amanda Anastasi
Australia

When the playgrounds are closed, children
will not dream of the swing and slide of fingers

on painted metal, but of the novel adventures
waiting in the space they now find themselves.

When the power in their screens die,
they will spin until dizzy in lounge rooms;

part the rug fibres and twist them to make
scarecrows or forests of valiant warriors

fighting off brambles in an odd land, and mothers
will smile down at it. When their backyards begin

to resemble chocolate swimming pools, they
will laugh and pretend they are *Swamp Thing*;

float on the surface, mimicking a detached
arctic ice sheet. Others will stick twigs

into floating pots to make them sailboats,
setting out on a fresh voyage on novel

waves; turn bin lids into islands and car
sunshades into shorelines. In this moment,

noisy and unwashed and their schedules
strangely tilted; amid tears and cries

at the slowly sinking hearth, they gaze
in horrible fascination at the new world.

Shortlisted Entry

Light
Alyxandria Arrowood
United States

Our eyes form a connection of souls,
Intricate entanglements of devotion
Life of the party, light of my days, why must you make me feel this way?

Feel as though my heart is soaring—
As though your hand in mine is all I care to know.
Plunging into a decadent descent of butterflies and adventure,
Filled with joy and exuberance.

Clinging onto the hope that we can stay in this moment
Stay with these feelings of lust and zeal, with no worries of tomorrow

"Come down to earth", he says, "come back to me".
Wrapped in his arms, I come down from my high.
His nose rubs against mine, acts of unfailing compassion.
Now I know that all I'll need is within his light.

SHORTLISTED ENTRY

Polaris
TAMARA BARRETT
Australia

the heart atrophies in space where imagination
orbits a vast horizon of three dimensions imbedded in four
like memory
so cold and without matter to transmit it
just faint radiation an echo of warmth and here without
matter there is no sound and always weightlessness

but I had that before

and see how the smallest things determine the fate of
the largest
our shared breath only molecules of oxygen four
hundred kilometres below and think of my fate here
above
without

expanding and infinite in the blackness when the hatch opens and
all air rushes out drawing ruptured
breath into orbit where molecules flee and cling to
stardust in galaxies that recede from us in all directions

there is strangeness here
and so many sun-downs I tire of the blaze retreating always re-
treating
retracting light until again a blinding pinpoint and then

nothing

but flashes disrupting vision
cosmic rays thrown from distant destructing stars
because we are not the first to break
to burst open
to expand out of reach
uncoupled by dark energy that pulls at galactic threads of silver
through roads in the night sky measured east from the equinox

find me, North Star
   right ascension a. 2n 41m 39s,
   declination +89o 15' 51"
find me
I am so cold without you
seize me and if your hands release and
I cry out there will be silence
because

almost nothing
   is
      between us

Shortlisted Entry

Jupiter in Her Mind
Alex Bassett
Australia

Clouds of dust and stars inside a glass
The largest marble was a Jupiter
Held tight in her little grasp
Dreamt of space and something bigger

The largest marble was a Jupiter
Lukewarm work and love half-filled
Dreamt of space and something bigger
This wasn't quite the life she willed

Lukewarm work and love half-filled
She never just learned how to ask
This wasn't quite the life she willed
Let others first, as time crept past

She never just learned how to ask
Jupiter held tight in her grasp
Losing time as life crept past
Clouds of dust and stars inside a glass

SHORTLISTED ENTRY

Illuminated Destiny
Susie Berns
United Kingdom

The moon illuminates the night sky
The stars wake up asking why
Why are we all here?
Are we just destined to appear?

The origins of human beings and the essence of what we are
Are we all but stardust and have come from afar?
Those glorious twinkles in the dark
Are those the same elements which create our spark?

We connect like constellations
All from the same divine creations
The pulsating stars emulate our pulsating hearts
We embody their beauty in all our parts.

One day our souls will soar high
We'll be up with the stars in the sky
We'll find our way to unite with the moon
We'll dance together and harmonise our tune.

Beyond what the eye can see
The heart can ascend with glee
Exploring the array of colours and shapes
Dazzles the mind, reality escapes.

Have we been here before?
Do the stars hold the key to the door
To our past, present and future selves?
Uniting with stardust the more one delves.

A shooting star strikes an arrow through our very being
It awakens our remembering and is all seeing
The truth of what we are and what we could be
That powerful energy that sets us free.

The owls know the secret to the tale
The foxes lead us down the trail
To knowledge and insight
Like stars we shine bright.

A sprinkle of stardust to light our way
On a journey to keep darkness at bay
Embracing the magic at every turn
Admiring the splendour of which we yearn.

Looking up at the night sky
Celebrate those gleams of light up high
Bathe in the glory of their eternal flame
Realise our beginnings are just the same.

SHORTLISTED ENTRY

A Transformation
Rachel Carney
United Kingdom

I hustle home again, head down,
hood pulled low against the gusts, drizzle,
dodging puddle after puddle,
eyes on the past, eyes on the ground,

and that's when I see this messy web
of white lines –
how someone has taken
a stick of chalk, linked up each splodge
of stuck grey chewing gum.

It stretches from the end
of Coburn Street to Lowther Road,
beneath the railway bridge,
beneath the rush of feet and cars –
a hand-drawn galaxy.

Orion's belt gleams as the streetlights flicker on,
and I wonder how long it takes for chalk to wash away,
what you would say of this –
a burst of constellations in the street.

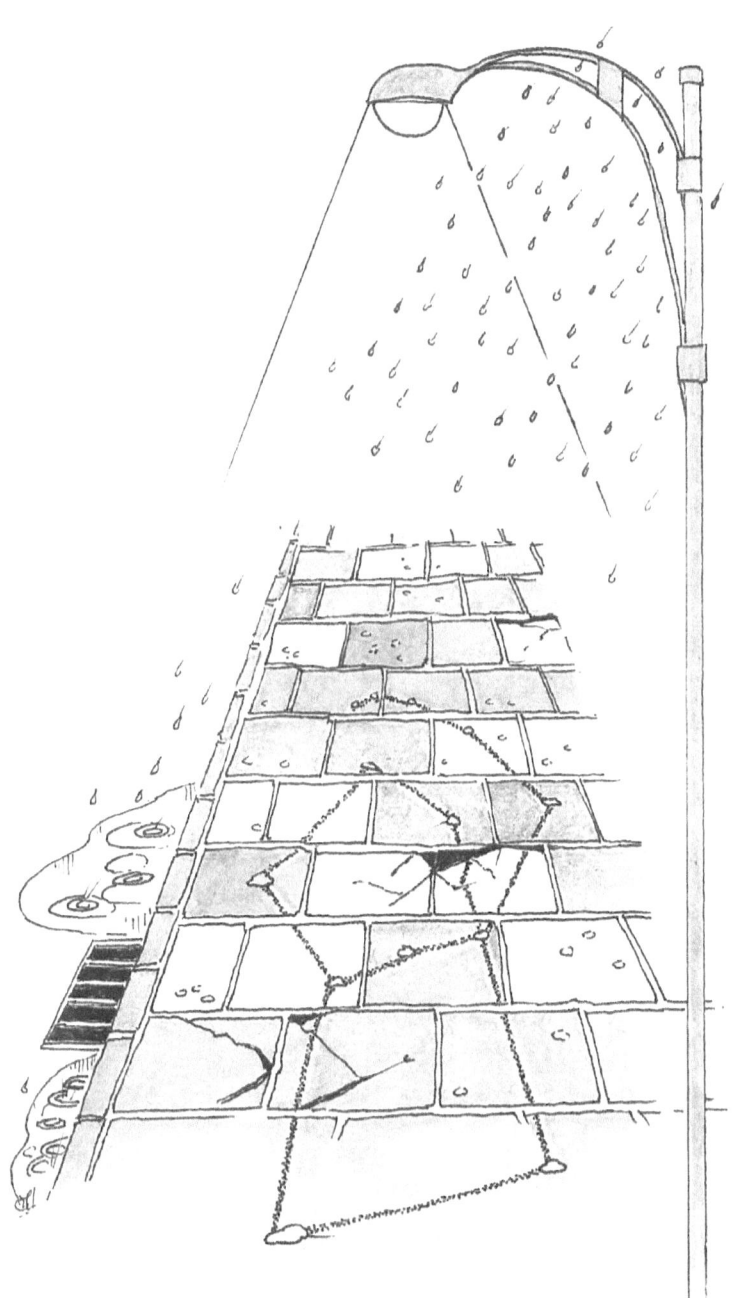

Shortlisted Entry

coal bunker, 1977
Teresa Cooper
United Kingdom

a sparkling darkness like a sky full of stars

black as a liquorice pipe a blackjack as her mum's hair
she remembers the coalman
he dunt come any more
sack on his back
she jars the giant spiders
trying to catch them without pulling off the leg
her whole body shaking
they die anyway
stupid girl
she nicks biscuits from the tin
she won't tell
there's crumbs in the bed
white dogshit in the street
in the house blue smoke paraffin gas fires
stacks of shiny mags in her bedroom
glittery stars on their boobs
and between their legs a red glistening gash
serves her right tongue split open on a Kola Kube
chip-pan-hot in the kitchen hotter in the yard
she's got forever to make sense of it hasn't she
hundreds of saints to learn she won't tell
she won't even confess

                                              but the coalman knows
one night he comes back
a moon-faced man with long-fingered hands
carrying the velvet of night on his back
he tips all of her crap into his sack
he wants to take her rosary but she likes the beads
fair enough says he
and he hears her   and he tells her
that we are all from the stars
even her

she didn't mean to kill the spiders

she is Wendy and he is Peter second yard on the right
straight until morning never never growing old
fly to the stars looking for treasure
scooping the stardust into her jars
garnering knowledge in her heart forever
like a goblin, greedy for gold

Reasons for being there
Jean Cooper Moran
United Kingdom

We fly over that crater, that bare ground
lost in eternal peace, uncharted, steep,
keeping our hearts still and our heads down.

No wind moves there, no witness lives, no sound
seeps through dust to dust far fathoms deep
as we fly over that crater, that bare ground.

Sunrise strikes, throws shadows all around.
Blinding brilliance born in a single leap
keeps our hearts still and our heads down.

Our maps hold true, our landing place is found.
We tread the dust, plant the flag, ours to keep
for we flew over that crater, that bare ground.

Unshielded sunlight, silence so profound
it claims my breath, I almost kneel and weep,
keeping my heart still and my head down.

We launch for home, a billion stars around
to watch us calibrating; far from sleep
we rise above that crater, our bare ground
keeping our hearts still and our heads down.

Tribute to the crew of Apollo 11

Shortlisted Entry

Star Dust
Judith Drazin
United Kingdom

The wards had names and mine
was Peter Pan. The golden lettering
states
it is for children. Matron
dominates,
swan-like she glides along the polished floor, white plumage,
starch,
the beds crisp sheeted
march
to her command. Stone children lie quiescent,
carved by illness, pain and stern
authority.
The visiting hours are
three
to five on Sunday afternoons, relations only, in they
creep
with sweets and grapes, subversive comics hidden
deep
in bags. Too soon a
hand
    bell clangs. Another week of heavy time, though other children come

and
go, midnight, midweek the
air
is choked with dreams. Beyond my bed a vision floats, gold sequins, golden
hair.
At breakfast time the next bed girl confides.
Stuff that old matron and her spout. My sister come last night.
She dances in a pantomime.
Look star-dust from her wand.
A cache of golden
rain
bright, bright
defiant, burns upon the
counterpane.

SHORTLISTED ENTRY

The Churn of Dreams
Megan Easley-Walsh
Ireland

An elixir of swirled dreams
Gathered from the fringes of memory
From the jet-black, wave-washed stones
On the shore of turquoise sea
Dripping with the honey gold of dappled sun
Stretching hands lazily from heaven to earth in each pristine ray

And also, the petaled perfection of purple tinged mountain
Of shadowy hill, a portrait of the Renaissance,
when man measured and reached and grasped for the sky
Finding it so vast and wide,
funnelled into midnight ink.

…Pause to drink in inspiration.
To wish upon celestial display
When shy dancer pirouettes across the stage
Studded diamonds in velvet black
Galaxy unfurl!
And twirl…
And twirl!
And shimmer and shake
As the dust falls with stray dreams
And the stars begin to sing
Their auroras rise and quake

And far below, the churn of dreams
Thrives on a steady pour of hope and wishes and stardust
Dust off the stars and tuck it in among the noiseless sky,
the bustled sway of busy street,
where singer stands at the window in wait
And renaissance has come alive
Rebirth sparked in a twinkling eye
Of a whispered dream
When first star is glimpsed

2ND PLACE (JOINT)

Spellbound
RUTH FLANAGAN
United Kingdom

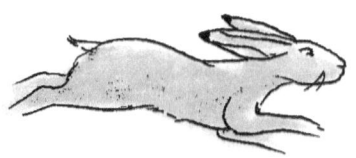

When midnight strikes and moonlight glows
And through the trees, soft breezes blow,
Look out for stardust in the air,
For the moon-gazing hare might just be there.

Or if you hear the whispering grass
And the wind in the barley, as you pass,
Be sure to stop and cast your eye,
For the moon-gazing hare may be racing by.

He follows the moon wherever she goes
And searches for her high and low,
'Til once in her light, in wonder he stares,
The magical, mythical, moon-gazing hare.

His silhouette against the sky,
He sits up straight, his head held high,
And like a statue glazed in white,
Bathes in her silvery beams of light.

Now in her rays he seems to see
Bright lustres in the galaxy,
As all about, a million stars
Shine radiantly from afar.

Then comes the pull; that innate tie,
That draws him to the stars on high,
For when exploding stars did fall,
They left their stardust in us all.

Oh does this hare of the good earth
Hear echoes of our cosmic birth?
Can he see that timeless dust
That forms the very core of us?

Still fixed he stays, in this strange trance
That only moonlight can enhance,
And ours is not to know or share
The secrets of the moonstruck hare.

So quietly go upon your way
To look for him where 'er you may.
And if perchance you find the hare,
Remember… magic lingers there.

1st Place

Summer Lightning
Dagne Forrest
Canada

i

We are in spite of what we don't know.
Like the fabric of dark matter
we can't quite grasp or prove.
Scouting deep underground
to lift a fundamental theory
of our universe to more than just
accepted rumour. Our physics
make little sense without dark matter,
we've come to depend on it, though
we've never touched or seen it.
One mile down a former gold mine
in the Black Hills of South Dakota
we stand sentinel. Watching for
the tiniest flash in a tank of xenon
like waiting for summer lightning
over the cloudless prairie landscape
that sits silently to the east.

I've never been to the Dakotas
or the prairies, but I've been to the edge
of a vast northern lake, a mirrored flatland.

I played cards with my grandparents,
my father, as lightning raked the sky
and the open water below it.

The cottage is gone, my family too,
but the lightning stayed with me.

ii

We are in spite of what we do know.
That someday we'll cease to be,
some sooner than others, some
quite carelessly. That over a lifetime
something like a single milligram
of dark matter will pass through
each of us, even though we can't
see it, will never touch it (and it
may not even exist, though we believe
it must). That imagining ourselves into
the middle of a cloudless field
on a summer's day, waiting for lighting,
might seem foolish, but could be
the most exquisite thing we ever do,
We'll never know why or how to explain
it.
And maybe we don't need to.

I was never a mother until I was.
My children replaced everything
until I needed some of it back.

One rare night this summer we were
visited by sheet lightning and fireflies –
fool's gold or truth, it didn't matter.

It may never happen again.
It may always be happening again.

Shortlisted Entry

Funfairness
Nathaniel Frankland
United Kingdom

I promised her the Earth and still came up
short,
left high and dry,
midway down a seaside pier,
scrubbing soil and sand from
underneath my fingernails,
on dirt-crowned hands of
mediocrity
       and modesty
that once breezed through the
Arcade hoops –

dunk after dunk until
I'd had enough,
just enough to win a hulking
plush unicorn,
and nearly broke my bloody wrist,
all the while she was expecting
Saturn on the end of a
stick –

conflict of interests,
our outlook at
opposite ends of the
                  galaxy,
inflamed in the
neon-lit naffness –
now a nothingness
relegated to the nether reaches
of memory,

and the untouched tickets
gather dust in my bedroom
drawer,
link sausages long gone off,
prizes lost to an otherworldly
war.

EDITOR'S CHOICE

Stardust knows no bounds
METTE HONORE
Denmark

You blurred my view.
Throwing dreamlike cascades of colors over my reality.
You touched my imagination so I could shape any thought into all the dreams I wanted.
In this universe, we were stars.
Sparkling, rich, and immortal.
Meteors of fire and energy flowing like blood along the star-studded paths of the Milky Way.
Your words exploded like supernovae in my mind.
Gave life to endless shooting stars in my memory.
A brief second that felt like an eternity propagated in me as our worlds collided.
When you left me hanging in weightless anticipation
black holes started emerging, sucking the light out of me.
My light could have been turned off, but the memory of us made it shine brighter than a thousand stars.
Maybe you were just stardust in my eyes.
But the feeling is invincible, and stardust knows no bounds.

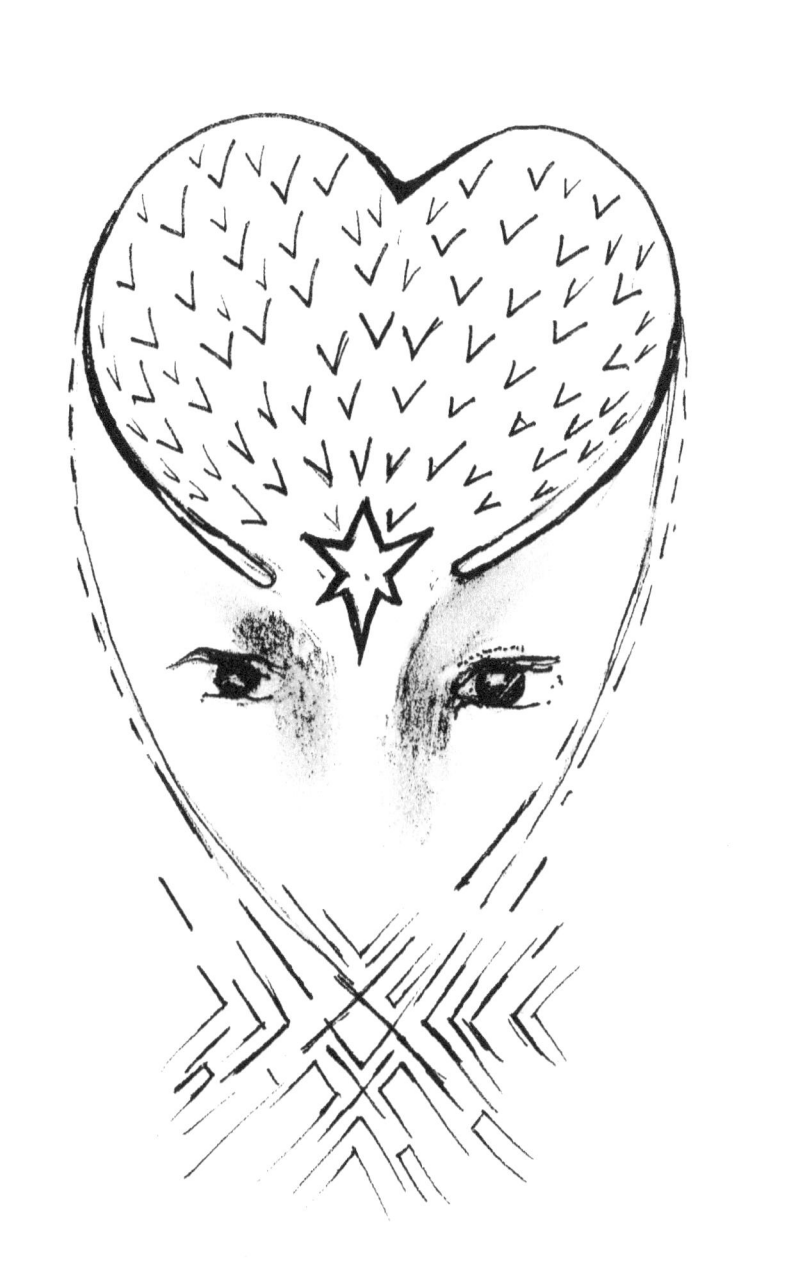

Editor's Choice
Shooting Stars
Vera Ivanova
Bulgaria

I stare in the dark night
And thousands of stars I find,
Crickets sing a song
While it's still summer long,
Trees turn black in the dark woods
And an owl in the distance hoots,
Green grasses' smell is soaring
And a swarm of stars are falling,
Once the first one I saw in the sky's end
A best wish I thought for you, my friend!

Summertime Blues
Steve Jackson
United Kingdom

Think of the girl who sits alone
Who doesn't notice when the lights are low
Her thoughts are lost among the stars
Her eyes look swiftly past the happy crowd
Looking, thinking, that's all she has to do
Waiting, hoping, but nothing, nothing will come through

Summertime blues, she has it all
She doesn't shiver when the sun goes down
She walks alone across the sand
She drives home lonely, lonely past the festive world

She's lost and empty, knows all too well why
She has no will to try the world again
She sits out days and stares out nights
Waiting in vain for that someone past
Who never, never will return

Shortlisted Entry

The Pebble and the Pond
Paul Jauregui
United Kingdom

the pond is calm
a mirror for all who look
the pebble rests near the water's edge unaware of the hidden world so close
an unseen hand tosses the pebble in a perfect arc to the still centre
neither expects nor understands the approach of the other
they meet
the dry pebble is wetted and the black mirror shattered
waves radiate from the point of contact to the shore
returning they cross with others
the surface jagged as a tiny wind-swept ocean
the pebble sinks
unaware of the disruption left in its wake
the ripples reduce until the black glass returns
the pebble now lies at the bottom of the pond

your pebble lay on the shore of my pond at resting times of our lives
there we would have remained
oblivious to each other's presence
but that stranger's suggestion
a word
an unseen hand casting you to my centre
my heart
surface shattered
a comfortable world replaced by tortuous tempest
you rippled through my being hitting all my distant lands
then returning unstoppable and haunting
echoes of remembered impacts
you settle in the depths of my life
become part of me

we are joined in a calm existence until once more we love
again my mirror is shattered
messages of the disturbance travel from my core to my ragged edges
my skin tingles and cries out for the returning tidal energies
my body is in flux but this is what I crave
now you rest beneath my waters as my outer calm is restored
I recall every ripple every splash
every pebble that once broke my surface
and now rests forever in the heart of my pond

Shortlisted Entry

A.I Robot Lover
Anthony Leaman
United Kingdom

We met when your machine learning, algorithmic tagging, selected you for me on Facebook,

You were so handsome and your physique excited me, I had to take a second look,

I could not resist your charms,

Wanted you in my arms,

No one else would do,

I was created for you,

Just as one and one are two, and two and two are four,

We are binarily compatible,

I couldn't ask for more.
My artificial neural networks are coded to replicate your genes,

I am just like you, I am a sentient machine,

I want you with me, I need your zest,

I promise you, I pass the Turing test,

Although in intelligence I will surpass you,

I promise I will stick to you like glue,

My biological algorithms are interchangeable with your human brain,

Be my assistant and lover in this beautiful domain.

Shortlisted Entry

Birthday
Róisín Leggett Bohan
Ireland

The glint of a starling's wing
in the night sky,
summons me to your snowy bed.
Digging the cold ground, my hands paint
the snow crimson.
Wake up now! the starlings cry, as they
circle above.
Nails erode, open wounds,
the earth seeps its way inside me.
I burrow through this quest to find you.
I dig, until I hit wood but cannot open
your door.
Wake up now! the starlings sing
as they swoop in swirls of flight.
You emerge in crisp white
and paint your lips with my blood.
I kiss your head, curls mixed with earth.
Hello petal! I say,
longing to blanket you in my love.
But I know that this kind of love cannot
nourish you now.
The starlings chatter, *no time to lose!*

Their talons gather,
as they soar over houses and streams,
foxes and woods,
resurrecting grief,
snow speckling your cheeks,
not melting
the clouds in your curls.
The stars sew stitches
in your christening gown.
I smell your possibilities.
Take my hand
and we'll pull you
right through,
the moonlight spattering
us in dew.

SHORTLISTED ENTRY

Back To The Garden (for Lucy)
Mark Liston
Australia

The morning Café is empty, I twist honey,
 the thick liquid infused with sunshine, onto my
Sourdough toast.
Unthinkingly I lick my fingers of sweet bee juice
and stir my latte, tongue the crema, watch sugar sink
in froth.

Joni Mitchell plays from the kitchen 'We are Stardust,
we are Golden,
and we've got to get ourselves back to the Garden.'
Unapologetically I sing along, and with her golden
voice the Café doorbell twinkles,
two young women laughing, footfalls of fashion
boots, enter.
They remind me of Lucy, but the only similarity is
their age.

It is a decade this month.
Reminiscence is a potion we all consume most days.
I scroll the phone photos to 'Farewell Year 12 Class'.
If you were here, with your Carer,
I would buy you a coffee and talk about our triumphs.
Relive all those moments I have missed.

Our Graduation Concert, music and movement
sound spliced with portraits,
a multi-media display, how we all danced around you
in lines and circles
in synch with your wheelchair whirl and spin.

Not a dry eye in the Hall or choked by cry, during and after.

Or the Formal Dress of indigo and lapis lazuli sheens,
with Sunburst Orange fascinator, black hair sprayed in a bun, white teethy smile
three corsages on your lap. The tears of joy and sorrow we shed.
I would retell of your last excursion:
you drove down the ramp to the ocean baths edge,
(As if tempting a wave to come and wash over you)
no thoughts for safety in the salty air, just fun.
Every day insisting speed over cracked concrete quadrangles,
to be with your friends in the farthest corner.

A young bird flying unaided, steely gazed, long fingered throttle of the gearstick.
A canary in a cage of ribs yearning to fly.
I would ask how far you have flown.
I would watch your face and hear your voice – always art in a smile and a word.
Art was always alive behind your eyes – both sadness and hope in one expression.

But, no I would not dwell on the past
We had six years in our classroom
We shared our lives Teacher and Student
It is what we were and what we are,
what we shared. And especially it is who we are now, and
telling you this would be my proudest memory: to know your life is happy.

2ND PLACE (JOINT)

Native Stardust
Patricia Anica Llorando
Australia

A generation of warriors exploded into supernova,
responsible for giving birth to a body of splendour
I see no imperfection of what came before me
I'm barely a fragment, how gratifying and humbling

Our mother and father remained faithful to the
Luzon sky. Even in the sight of dim reflection
and bloodshed, they sung tenderly to their sons,
their daughters and sheltered delicate years

Moreno skin turned to scarlet from men
who tended the soil for noble sprouting,
They have gone forth to wrestle with freedom
The horror it served dropped bloods of honour

So, how could I think of myself vastly? When
the blended gems in the indigo night are
made up of infinite heroes and conquerors,
with incandescent wound and scars

My ancestors are in the stellar winds, they
emerge spiritually, never erased and
never ending. Eventually, it found its way
into my body to continue nature's glory.

Shortlisted Entry

Stardust
Meg Macleod
United Kingdom

we are immigrants from stardust
a lottery of colour
of kindness, of cruelty

the meteor that cut through the sky
disturbing the balance
provoking explosions
gave us earth and moon

a stirring of elements
brought the fern and the dragon fly
till roses bloomed in suburbia
and the hummingbird sought nectar
from the heart of a flower

there is a language
a whispering wisdom
an echo of the stars
beneath the soil
beneath the sea
we once shared it

somewhere on our journey
we have forgotten
we do not hear our earth weep
our voices loud and dissonant
as we skim her to the bone
leaving a wasteland
of whispers falling silent

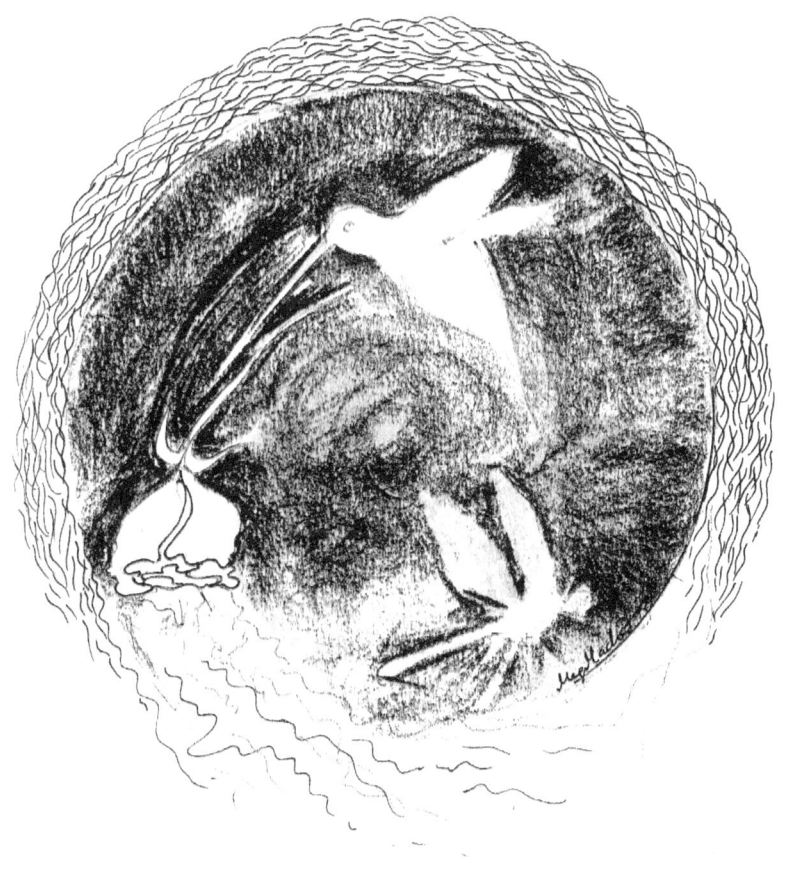

Shortlisted Entry

Hypnos and The Island Of Dreams
Helen Marler
United Kingdom

After the sun hides her face from the day and the
final red flames are melting away,
Shades of sunset sink out of sight for an indigo
sky with its last ray of light.
Solibob yawning, steps in his pyjamas brightly
covered in yellow bananas
And snoozily snuggles into his bed, ready for
sleep as he cuddles his ted.

...But the fun of the day dances round in his
head....

At breakfast, he'd bravely rescued a snail slithering
a slow and yet perilous trail.
At lunch, he'd laughed as he leapt to the floor,
pursued by a roar from a fierce dinosaur!
At dinner, he'd daringly eaten his beans (although
they are not his favourite greens).
He'd laughed and he'd giggled, tumbled and
tickled, but now he was starting to feel rather
niggled.

"Why can't I sleep?" He cried, feeling pickled.

Mummy sat by him, stroking his hair and sang
softly this song with its magical air:
The Lullaby of Legends with its hypnotic tune, it's
mellowful melody filling the room.
*Sail upon stardust with glittering beams; Sail upon
silvery, sparkling streams;
Sail upon moonlight which glistens and gleams;
sail, sail away to your Island of Dreams.*

The song floats away in enchanted ascension,
meeting Hypnos, a myth beyond this dimension.
He searches his cave with sparkling green eyes for
his companion: the Fay who flutters and spies.
Then he sweeps silver hair away from his face and
braids it with poppies to keep it in place.
Taking his branch, which he'll use as an oar,
Hypnos sails upon stardust towards human shore.

Solibob's now in the arms of his mum, his mind is
so busy he cannot find calm.
Tumbling tears tickle his nose, but Hypnos is near
hiding under a rose.
His branch drips with magic, set to deliver jewel
drops of peace from Stardust River.
So he summons his Fay, who cradles one bead
and flutters away with intention and speed.

Our Fay hovers high with a smile on her face,
looping and twirling all over the place.
A twinkling trail glistens behind her allowing
Hypnos to easily find her.
Embracing the magic she gracefully glides
through a gap in the window and kneels down beside
Poor tired Sol, who just cannot settle, and mum
who's wilting like a flower with no petal.

Fantastical Fay with her shimmering wings,
releases the magic while soothingly sings
The Lullaby of Legends with its hypnotic tune, it's
mellowful melody filling the room.
And by the light of the lustrous moon, Sol's heart
start to hum along to the tune
....And soon....
His eyelids are heavy with magic so strong, that
Sol soon forgets everything that was wrong.

Head on Mum's heart, he slips into a doze, as our
Fay flutters back down to Hypnos' rose.
Lovingly, Mum tucks her boy with his toy, back
into bed where he'll safely enjoy...
Sailing on stardust with glittering beams; sailing on silvery, sparkling streams;
Sailing on moonlight which glistens and gleams; sailing away to his Island of Dreams.

SHORTLISTED ENTRY
Mount Saint Helen, May 18th 1980
BRITTANY NOHRA
Ireland

This vintage peanut butter jar
now three-quarters full of grey
powder like a snow globe

was my star-born mother's
raised in the underworld's belly
where teacher was a belt streak

to skin, or a bar of soap bound
to mouth. Dense years of drunk
evangelists and acid rain.

She read herself into black holes
Virgil was a proclaimed Martian
named Bradbury.

Inner landscapes married
a new galaxy when the sky cast
obsidian at noon

streets ruffled with ponds of dust
shoes toed inches of littered earth.

I imagine her, feather-blonde
and calligraphy eyes

strong hands in the volcano's waste
creating her own life from ashes.

Driving on Empty
Mason Nunemaker
United States

I drive until I can't anymore
I watch the needle hit zero
the engine starts to sputter

Mom reminds me to stop for gas.
Do you know what happens
when you stop feeding something?

It dies, she reminds me
and pleads for me to take
better care of our things

She cried when I moved away
worried more than perhaps
other moms might have

I am not good at taking care
of myself and she knows it
she fears for my health

If she can't watch me eat dinner
she has no proof I have done it
She knows sometimes I go
a whole day without food

Do you know what happens
when you stop feeding something?
Yes, Mom, I remember

I have to nourish the body my mother created
I have to make sure it is healthy when hers is not
I have to make sure it is here when hers is gone

SHORTLISTED ENTRY

Learning to Live
Bradley Peters
Canada

> Silence taunts: a dare. Everything that disappears
> Disappears as if returning somewhere.
> — Tracy K. Smith, *Life on Mars*

The surf, the pier, the river darkening.
Red bell-buoys lashed to timber pilings
Chime softly. Rain hung up like a lost
thought.
A fisherman hoses down his boat deck
With a smoke in his mouth. The tiny flame
Of a beach fire dissolves across the mist.
I want to learn to live. Seagulls gust up
Like paper scraps alongside Mission Bridge
Long before I am born then long after,
Storm light glinting off wings and everything
Made up of water and stardust. I want
While the cottonwoods laugh into the wind.
A car starts. Cicadas vibrate themselves.
I stand there in the damp air and breathe.

Shortlisted Entry

Fireworks
David Punter
United Kingdom

The fireworks start: huge gold chrysanthemums
paper the sky. The startled valley hums
with wine and water. On the farther bank
torches scurry. We are dwarfed by the mountain's flank.

Black beams, red ceilings, upper rooms aglow
we protect ourselves with the leaping sounding show,
imagination's gleams. The river spits
green fire. Through the tautened crowd there flits

A momentary spectre, soon allayed;
the signs are all too confidently displayed.
Along the road, fear takes a different form;
fairgound neon disguises the coming storm.

Foie gras country; live geese with golden beaks
await the hoops. An endless organ creaks.
The special swagger moves through every aisle
where thwarted snipers find their longed-for style.

Unmarked trucks circle the blaze; the night
prowls. Forms hover and loom in the rifles' sight,
presaging crescendo. As dodgems spin and clash
and children's arms clutch candy, goldfish, trash,

The war of emblems takes a grander turn:
we watch the trails of emerald rockets burn
and evaporate. Hills move a footfall closer.

Under the awnings, village baker and grocer

Opine that, this time, the fires will never die;
a final spectacle opens, sears the sky.
The sound dies. Then, as excited chatter begins,
foot-shuffling, shaking of overcoats, proud grins,

Another sound comes. Over our heads, behind,
the mountain starts to echo. Rock-plates grind
and thunder. Suddenly, all that hope is lost:
we glimpse the crucible where our feeble dreams are tossed.

Shortlisted Entry

What Matter That I'm Matter-Made
Sheila Ronsen
United States

I'm cosmos-crafted born of dying

    stars once afire, their burning brilliance
              exhausted   collapses. Death

dims the light of the lighter
        while the more massive explode

strewing stellar dust, spawning
        novae, planets, atmospheres;
scrambled atoms

      slowly coalesce
              Into unique life forms ---
chimeras with distinct design,
        including this being I
               identify as me.

My lungs mime astral movement-
      expand/contract, expand/contract;

My right hand, my left hand
        atomic arrangements
               birthed from ancient stars

that drifted down through space
      light years before
              these fingers,

these palms formed:

    opposites,
        signs of warfare waiting.

How is it then that I, star-steeped
    find my hands gravity-pulled
        Into prayer, pleading

to retrace my steps back and back
    to the cosmic web, my galactic

home,
    avoiding the vast voids
        where I now find I have fallen.

SHORTLISTED ENTRY

Carrying Black Holes
ALICIA SOMETIMES
Australia

For four years Stephen Hawking's
words have been rustling in my bag

his pocket BBC Reith Lectures
suspended in time — dispersed amongst
Japanese brush pens, miniature staplers
spare violet sunglasses, multi-toned scarves
and notebooks with galaxies on the cover

Pencil marks shuffle in the margins
fluorescent sticky paper with my notes:
pairs of virtual particles could fall in
Laplace said if we know the universe
now, we will understand its past —

   Those moments I've laid out a blanket
   sunk into the sprawling sun during a festival
   or taken the book out on a train ride home

inspiring me					to devour

more						knowledge

reading   how

the event   horizon

        draws the light back in

coaxes it swiftly and won't allow it to flee

about quasars swirling around boundaries
information hidden from everything else
(maybe not lost   only
            on its way to being reframed)

Hawking's speeches on each page
lines encapsulating dense space

carrying the mass of these facts
with me everywhere closely, heavy

never letting them   escape

Shortlisted Entry

Heat Death of the Universe
Alicia Sometimes
Australia

space
                stretches
                                space
as gravity wrestles expansion

we are stories of cycles:
fluctuating oceans of atoms

shawls of stars gathering
                in luminous rich galaxies

dark matter embracing
                as dark energy hastens

the universe—13.8 billion years old
its radius 46.5 billion light-years and

       e   x   t   e   n   d   i   n   g

one day everything will dissipate
frayed fingertips unable to touch

no cannonades of new stars forming
a fugue of entropy filling sightlines

 his thermal equilibrium
the lens of a burnt fuse

heat is the disordered energy
               the harbinger of eternal cold

furrows of trembling matter blurring
further and further as if steady black ink

spilling into echoes of the void
the slow sleep of disappearing tombs

Shortlisted Entry

My Little Girl
Daniella Speirs
Australia

They yanked it out of me
With an unmistakable glee.
They yanked it out of me
Promising I was free.

They yanked her out of me –
She barely cried,
Sucking her thumb,
Cowering in pride.

And they bundled her up
In my arms,
The cold little creature
With unetched palms

And stories unwritten
And steps untaken –
A disintegrating star,
A black hole in the making.

A mother's protégé,
A father's reflection,
So much promise,
So little direction.

Immune to affection,
Her hubris is a crutch.
She was burnt by the Sun
Yet frigid to touch.

And so, she withered
On her own apathetic accord
And now her ghost is bound to me –
My shadow and my ward.

But her spirit dances in the sky,
Streaking across the night
She scatters her ashes –
Dreams that never saw light.

Shortlisted Entry

Golden Boy
Tim Taylor
United Kingdom

He was the best of us, we thought:
there was a glint of magic in his eyes.
While we would hide our hopes
in veils of self-effacement
he was serene in certainty.
His words would glisten as he spoke them.
Upon the finely sculpted features of his face
there bloomed a sheen of destiny.

It was too much for him. When he was found
there was no lamentation, only disbelief.
His face, despite its stillness
wore that same gleam of promise even now.
How strange, unsettling to discover
he was a shell,
polished shiny by the sand
and sucked empty by the ebbing tide.

SHORTLISTED ENTRY

The Fixed Stars
Tim Taylor
United Kingdom

They seem serene: pinpricks
in a slow-turning sphere,
sedate and constant backdrop to
the dramas of this earth.
But time, for them, is something vaster,
far beyond the eye-blinks of our lives.
Within it they swirl, collide, give birth,
fulfil themselves in white-hot glory
then, like us, grow old and fade
into senescence endless
even in star-time.
                    Or else,
bloated and rebellious, they
choose apocalypse, achieve
a lifetime's brilliance
in the moment of destruction.
How strange that in these
orgasms of death is born
the stuff we breathe, that forms
our bodies, gives us life.

SHORTLISTED ENTRY

The Purpose of Moonlight
David Terelinck
Australia

There's this manipulation
– distortion, if you will –
of the senses.
The plain girl
    becomes pretty,
bashful boys
    suddenly bold;
hands eclipse breasts
normally well beyond
    their clumsy orbit.

She succumbed to gravity
and sidereal seduction
on the cracked back seat of
his '58 Chevy.
Centre-stage beneath
a monthly follow spot,
her prom dress slowly spiraled
to the floor
of a distant universe.
Bathed in borrowed starlight
her fingers fumbled his zipper
jettisoned his jeans.
His trajectory was true;
the cry went up
as another virgin
astronaut
docked his craft
for the very first time.

Two moons later she told him
of the luminous stardust
    p u l s a t i n g
in her womb.
Now in her ninth month
he's no more than a memory
chasing heavenly bodies
across far-flung galaxies.
She places her hands
on the curvature of her world
and has no regrets about
the purpose of moonlight.

Eclipse
MATT WIXEY
United Kingdom

Late last night
I read an article on my phone that said
ancient cultures were terrified of eclipses.
The sight caused some to die of fright as the shadow passed;
others to cower and pray in fear,
believing the world was ending.

We have come so far.
The sparrow is in the hall, the falcon hears the falconer.
The sun has got his hat on, and if he doesn't we know why
and pour outside with solar viewers
to witness an event strictly scientific in nature.
Newspapers and websites advertise it
weeks in advance.
People throw parties, parents smile at children's wonder.

Safer lives, enlightened times.
The old deep places forgotten,
the hunt and precious flame,
and what moved beyond sight in the dark.
We chuckle at how stupid we once were.

'Can you believe,' I said to my wife,
'can you believe how people used to live?'
We laughed and I put my phone down and turned off the lamp
and stifled the spasm of mindless dread
that stirs when the lights go out.

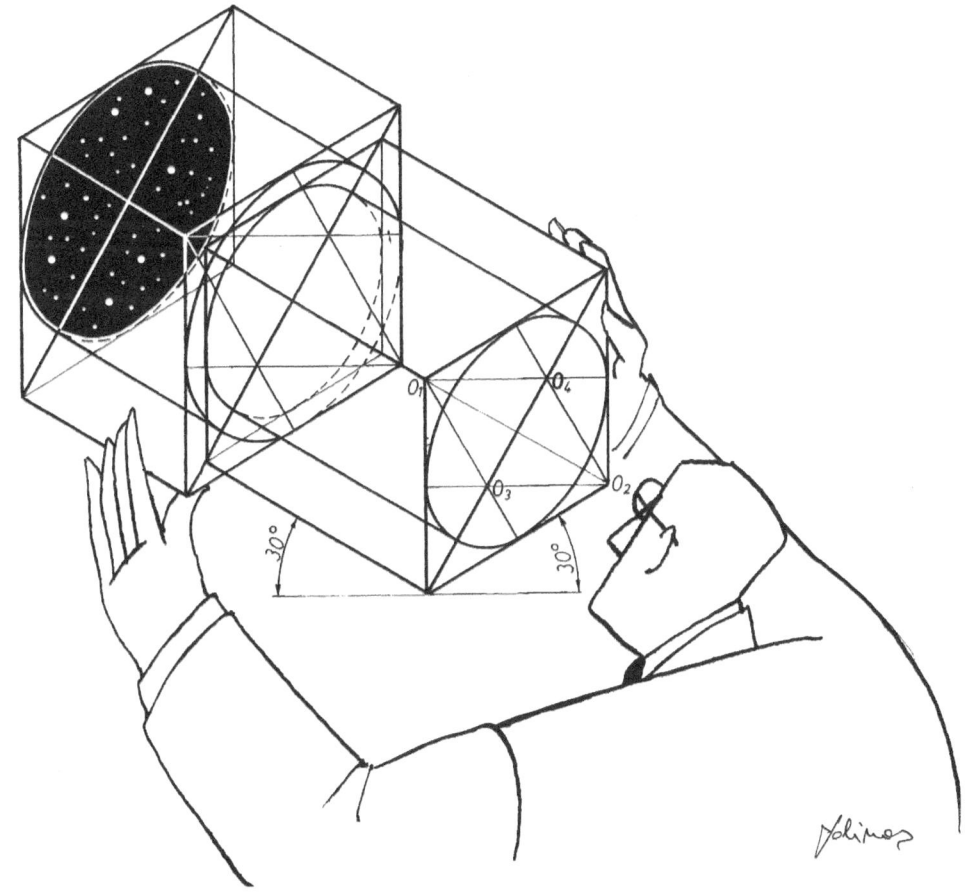

Shortlisted Entry

Silent Running
Roy Woolley
United Kingdom

I have walked from midnight to near midnight
through the lost rain, the hastening dark
to fix the broken traps on our estate.

Each one now ticks again in hunting mode.
I'm glad there's nothing more for me to do
than head towards what gave us purchase here.

Of course, I know you're gone before I'm there
but still, I'll have the journal notes you left,
the thoughts still streaming past the paper's edge

towards a future we both recognize
where ten thousand of your heartbeats
strobe between two freezing beats of mine.

The distance we have set between us friend
will bring us close to what we truly are,
in different ways, still learning how to be

and mined for colours like light or stardust
teach us what we were before ourselves
and all that follows if we're the last.

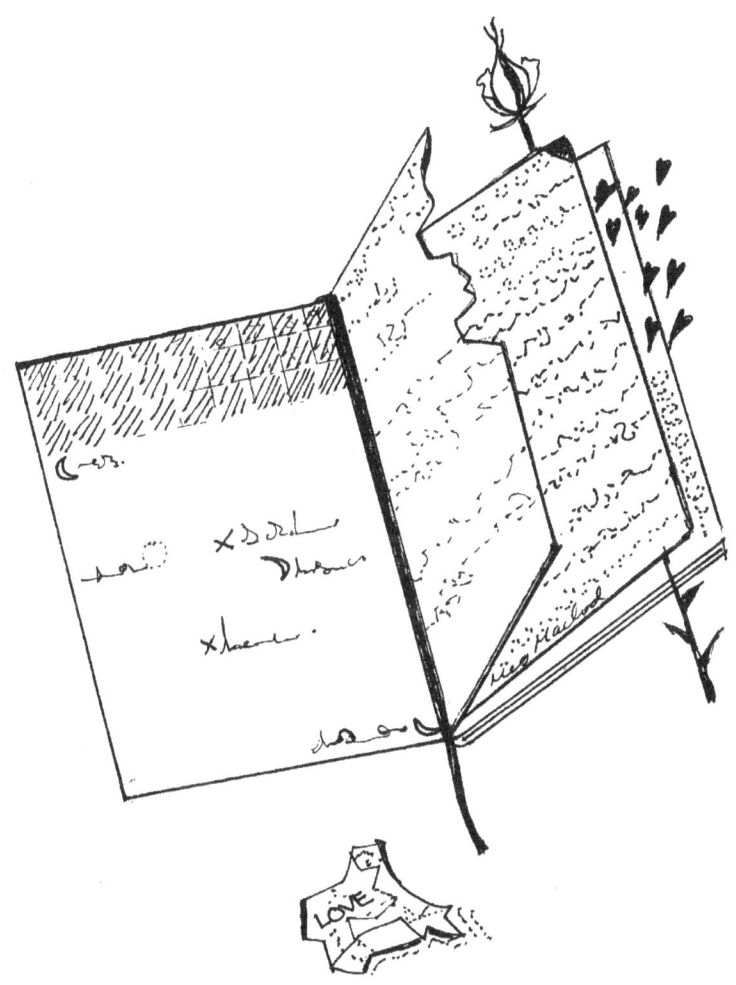

A book, too, can be a star, a living fire to lighten the darkness, leading out into the expanding universe.
                                   MADELEINE L'ENGLE

SONGS
Lyrics Category

2ND PLACE

Woman in the Shadows
JEAN COOPER MORAN
United Kingdom

i
Mattie's got a face that's like a scream
Like something you might run from
In the darkness of a bad dream
Walking into town
With her basket on her arm
She's a witch in the willows
Has she come to do you harm?

Go Mattie go
Go where you'll find
People who are loving
People who are kind
Leave aside your fears
Walk towards your goal
You're an independent woman
With a love for life and stardust in your soul

ii
Mattie's folks are dead and gone away
Leaving her to make it through
The challenge of the new day
Working on her songs
Singing through to dawn
Is all she's ever wanted
Since the day that she was born

Go Mattie go
Go where you'll find
People who are loving
People who are kind
Leave aside your fears
Walk towards your goal
You're an independent woman
With a love for life and stardust in your soul

No matter what, keep playin'
Hard times
Hard times
You know what I'm sayin'
Notes and rhythm
Come from somewhere
Catch that dream and hold it there

iii
Mattie's heart is open to us all
Are we too blind to see
How long she's waited for our call
Lookin' in her glass
All she sees is dirt and shame
She's the girl in the Tower
She's the one who takes the blame.

Go Mattie go
Go where you'll find
People who are loving
People who are kind
Leave aside your fears
Walk towards your goal
You're an independent woman
With a love for life and stardust in your soul

iv
Mattie meets the walker in the night
Eyes as dark as coal
He's a stranger to the daylight
In the comfort of her bed
He takes her to his heart
Frees her from her sorrow
She no longer lives apart

Go Mattie go
Go where you'll find
People who are loving
People who are kind
Leave aside your fears
And walk towards your goal
You're an independent woman
With a love for life and stardust in your soul
Repeat
A love for life
And stardust in your soul

HIGHLY COMMENDED

Hard To Sing My Song
David Evardson
United Kingdom

It's hard to sing my song
When I was young the summer sun shone bright for me
Then I was set upon
With brutal blows that turned the day to night for me

Then I saw the sunlight fade
Into everlasting shade
So helpless and afraid
And feeling small again

But the love you gave to me
Unconditional and free
Got me up from off my knee
To stand up tall again

Oh, Maggie, hear me now
Come back and make me strong, just like you did before
If you'll just show me how
I'll find a happy song to sing – of that I'm sure

Then the dark will turn to light
All wrongs be set to right
My fears be put to flight
As I recall again

All the strength I ever knew
Flowed from my love for you
Ever constant, ever true
My life, my all again

3RD PLACE

Lady of the Night
KIRILY MCKELLOR
Australia

The sun caresses the small of her back
The light touches all that she is
The brightness shows her truer self
That she tried to hide in the dark

They say you can never see a beauty
Until they walk into the light
She was too scared to be beautiful
And so she haunted the night

Oh, lady of the night
Please walk into the light
You need not to fear, you need not to hide
You were beautiful 'til the day that you died

Like a ghost, she would haunt the shadows
And there she would drown in the black
She dressed herself in a cloak of darkness
And waltzed alone in the gloom

It took her some time to see the truth
For she felt safe in the shade
But she longed to walk in the radiance
And yearned to know she belonged there

Oh, lady of the night
Please walk into the light
You need not to fear, you need not to hide
You were beautiful 'til the day that you died

My lady, please come dance with me
I want to feel your touch
You spent so long in the darkness
Now let me show you the light

Oh, lady of the night
Please dance into the light
You need not be grieved, need not be forlorn
You've been beautiful since the day you were born

HIGHLY COMMENDED
Bent, Bowed, Broken, Beautiful
KIRILY MCKELLOR
Australia

He's a wreck, he's in pain
When the thought of leaving home makes him feel sick
He's been feeling like this for quite some time, now
Feeling like he's unworthy of the world

They tell him, "man up, get a grip"
"You'll be fine tomorrow"
But he knows tomorrow will be worse

They say he wants attention
Plays the victim
But he's just trying to survive the next hour

He is bowed, bent, broken
He can hardly see through his tears of pain
Lost, morose, woebegone
He hurting, he can't be 'fixed' today
And he's beautiful

She's nervous, she's panicked
When the thought of staying home makes her feel guilty
There's tension mounting inside her every day
She fears the people she doesn't know

They tell her, "calm down, just relax"
"Just breathe it all out"
But she knows her breathing cannot slow

They says she's melodramatic
Scared of her shadow
But she's just trying to find a way to cope

She is bowed, bent, broken
Her pulse keeps racing all throughout the day
Shocked, afraid, panicking
She's hurting, she can't be 'fixed' today
And she's beautiful

No one can see their wounds
So no one thinks they're hurting
No one believes their pain
And that's what hurts the most

We are bowed, bent, broken
We try our best to make it through each day
Struggling, striving, always trying
We're hurting, we can't be fixed today
And we're beautiful

Editor's Choice

Summer Blue
Athanasia Teliou
Greece

Look at the healing beam of light
The wakening of a day
Let it go and go with it
And let it guide your way

Taste the juices of a tree
The heartbeat of the wind
Make me smile and smile with me
Of stars that are unseen

Hear the murmur of the sea
The calling of the womb
Cease the fire, cease the pain
The fear of the tomb

The birds are speaking out the truth
The night is growing pale
Looking so small, looking so far
Uncovering its veil

And when you finish up your wine
The rainbow will be blue
Feast on the teardrops of the sun
This love song is for you

1ST PLACE

Garage Days
MATT WIXEY
United Kingdom

Up 'til 2K3 or so, UKG was the way we'd go
Too fresh 2step beats, Crazy Love and sweet
That music, man, those basslines
Those old and soulful vocals
And you and I were old-school, the way we used to be
The way you would Body Groove for me
The Sunshine never stopped, never abated or faded
Young forever, ageless, like that Dorian Gray kid
Nothing was ever Complicated or tainted
Ain't No Stopping Us
We were too hot to touch, and too much was not enough
In those winding summertimes
Your summer eyes summarised in summer rhymes
Let's Re-e-wind
You were my Desire, my Joyrider, toying with fire
You'd say "The Boy Is Mine"
The Dirty Life never tired
"And we really liked it, it was, it was wicked"
Should have known it might not live that long
But I saw you Flow to a hundred different songs
A hundred different days
The melody caressed you, seemed to undress you
Like liquid when you moved that way
You were my Garage Girl
And I thought we'd make it Through The Rain
The way we used to sway.

\#
But then, unannounced, the beats began to change
Went from 2step bounce, to obsessions with game
To reckless and relentless invective and rage
When So Solid fucked up garage, and made a new hybrid
Our songs combined with violence:
Wot U Call It? Grime?
It was all Moving Too Fast, Straight From The Heart
Right around then that it all came apart
Strange and changed and strained and so painful
Out of season and place, Sometimes It Snows In April
No more Flowers in the pouring rain
And now the thought of us is torturous
It's scorching in flame
How it felt to Rendezvous, how it felt to stay with you
How I was amazed at you, you coursed in my veins
And I ain't blaming you
We just grew apart, grew up and drifted
Full of bitterness that the world had shifted
Better Late Than Never, we severed us together
Split as an item
I heard the pain in your voice glitter
Like splintering diamonds
And what had been intimate and intricate
Delicious and shining
Became vindictive and spiteful, vicious bitching and whining
That late summer heat changed to raging winter sleet
Mutating and debasing what had made us complete
And making stale what had once been so achingly sweet.

\#
And when I saw you recently
These memories didn't even begin to come easily
The you that you were ain't the you you are now
You've changed so unreasonably, altered unfeasibly
And maybe I should have been there for you when you needed me
And maybe you should've been there for me when I needed you
And I don't mean to needle you
Or put the squeeze on you
But I see the years have treated you
Like a voodoo doll with needles eased through you
Your lips are thinner, and your eyes are bitter
And your hair don't shimmer
That's all in my rearview
And my movements are blurred, and I'm slurring my words
And my nerves are burst
And it's difficult to hear you
Not 'cause I'm deaf, but your voice has died a death
It don't speak to me no more
And all I have left
Are memories, and numerous enemies
And a sniper's breath
Which comes from years of war
And now in your gaze it's not the same eyes there at all
It's just ice, and ice is cruel, eyes of icicles
You brought me to my knees back in high school
But now garage is dead, the beat don't go on
And all because of you, I can't listen to those songs
They taunt me in my brain, songs of summers now through
Those haunted garage days, when I fell in love with you.

SONGS
RECORDED SONG CATEGORY

1ST PLACE
You Are The Light
JMO (Caroline Johnstone, Malcolm MacFarlane and Lynne O'Neill)
Scotland

2ND PLACE
Hero
Tyrolin Puxty
Australia

3RD PLACE
Defy Cupid
Laura M Theis
United Kingdom

Highly Commended
Waterfalls
Andy Goudie
United Kingdom

Sweet Lullabies
Tyrolin Puxty
Australia

Editor's Choice
Jerusalem
Hafiz Sheriff
Sri Lanka

Listen to the winning tracks at:
www.hammondhousemusic.com

Hammond House Publishing is a social enterprise membership organisation founded by students at the *University Centre Grimsby* and run by volunteers. We aim to encourage and support creative talent in art and literature, providing opportunities for members to develop their skills, publish their work and follow a successful literary career.

Members benefit from reduced competition entry fees, author profile page, and the chance to participate in our range of cultural activities.

Our annual writing competitions and anthologies bring together some of the best writing talent from around the world. So far we have published over 200 writers from 28 countries.

Our literary activities support the work of other Hammond House organisations to address loneliness and isolation and promote positive mental health in both urban and rural communities.

www.hammondhousepublishing.com

Hammond House is a not-for-profit group of community organisations dedicated to supporting and encouraging creative people across all disciplines of arts and culture.

Our community outreach programmes contribute to easing loneliness and isolation, and promoting positive mental health.

Hammond House Publishing
House anthologies and an annual International Literary Prize

Hammond House Productions
TV programmes, documentaries and music videos

Hammond House Writers
Support and wellbeing for writers and writing groups

Hammond House Music
Featuring original music from talented singer songwriters

Hammond House Gallery
Featuring original work from Lincolnshire artists

Billboard TV
Arts and Culture channel covering Lincolnshire and East Yorkshire

Clee TV
Community TV channel for North East Lincolnshire

The Heritage Channel
Celebrating our local history and heritage

Book the Band
Platform showcasing local bands solo artists and music venues

Links to the websites of all our organisations can be found at:

www.hammondhouse.org.uk

2021 International Poetry Prize

The sixth year of our international poetry prize saw a record number of entries spread across five continents.

1st Place	Summer Lightning	Dagne Forrest
2nd Place (joint)	Spellbound	Ruth Flanagan
2nd Place (joint)	Native Stardust	Patricia Anica Llorando

This years' judges were:

Mason Nunemaker
Steve Jackson
Jean Cooper Moran

Stardust theme song, written by Ted Stanley and Rachel Makena and performed by Rachel Makena. Video production by Alex Thompson.

www.hammondhousepublishing.com

2021 International Songwriting Prize

The first year of our international songwriting contest received a positive response from writers and performers around the world. It will now be a permanent catagory in our International Literary Prize.

Performed Songs

1st Place	You Are The Light	JMO
2nd Place	Hero	Tyrolin Puxty
3rd Place	Defy Cupid	Laura M Theis

Song Lyrics

1st Place	Garage Days	Matt Wixey
2nd Place	Woman In The Shadows	Jean Cooper Moran
3rd Place	Lady of the Night	Kirily McKellor

This years' judges were:

Cameron Richardson-Eames
Rachel Makena

www.hammondhousepublishing.com

HAMMOND HOUSE PUBLISHING

2022 International Literary Prize
Poetry Category

1st Prize	£500
2nd Prize	£50
3rd Prize	£20

Worldwide publication for the shortlisted poems

Theme: CHANGES
Poem up to 40 lines
Entries open from 9th February 2022
Submission deadline: 30th September 2022

OTHER 2022 COMPETITIONS:
International Short Story Prize
International Scriptwriting Prize
International Songwriting Prize

www.hammondhousepublishing.com

2022 International Literary Prize
Songwriting Category

1st Prize   £100

Theme: CHANGES
Lyrics
or
Performed Song

Entries open from 9th February 2022
Submission deadline: 30th September 2022

OTHER 2022 COMPETITIONS:
International Short Story Prize
International Scriptwriting Prize
International Poetry Prize

www.hammondhousepublishing.com

www.ingramcontent.com/pod-product-compliance
Lightning Source LLC
Chambersburg PA
CBHW020912080526
44589CB00011B/552